# SPORT FOR ALL
# Tennis

**By Linda Dawson**
Illustrated by Liz Baranov

**CHERRYTREE BOOKS**

# Introduction

Tennis, or to give it its full name, Lawn Tennis, is a sport which is popular throughout most of the world – for players and for spectators. It is usually an outdoor sport, although there are increasing numbers of indoor courts as well.

One of the great attractions of tennis is that just about anyone can play – men and women, girls and boys of all ages, from those with the most basic skills to the very best. It combines plenty of good exercise with all the fun of a competitive sport in which you can pit your skills against your opponents.

Most people play tennis just for fun. For others though, such as those who play on the circuit of professional tournaments, tennis is a very serious matter and the most important aspect of their lives.

*Vigorous exercise, fresh air and the challenge of competition are what make tennis such a popular sport at all levels.*

Let us look at how the game is played, starting with the essential elements.

Two or four players can play in a tennis match. When two people play, this is called a singles match; when four people play, this is called a doubles match.

Tennis is played on a court which has been specially designed for the game, and which has a low net running across the centre. Players stand on either side of the net – in singles, one on either side; in doubles, two on either side.

Each player has a racket and hits the ball to his or her opponent. The basic aim of the game is to score points against your opponent by hitting the ball in such a way that he cannot return it to you.

*With four people on court, doubles matches can be great fun; to play doubles well you need all-round skills and good teamwork.*

3

# History

The game of Lawn Tennis originates from Real Tennis, or Royal Tennis, which was first played in France. It is thought that the word 'tennis' may have come from the way that early players of Real Tennis called out '*Tenez*!' (French for 'Get ready!') before serving the ball.

Real Tennis developed from the game of *Jeu de Paume*, which was a sort of hand-ball (the name means 'game played with the palm of the hand' in French). In early games of Real Tennis a glove was used to hit the ball. The first tennis rackets were developed from these gloves and were made of skin, or parchment, stretched over a wooden frame with a short handle. Later, people found that rackets made with gut strings were more effective.

The game of Real Tennis is played on an indoor court. The courts have roofed galleries to the side in imitation of the monastery cloisters where the game was first played. There are very few Real Tennis courts today, but there is a famous one at Hampton Court, near London, which was built for King Henry VIII in 1530, and where Real Tennis is still played.

*A game of Real Tennis: players can hit the ball against the walls or along the gallery roof. In this early version, the net is a simple cord with a fringe. Spectators can watch from the gallery.*

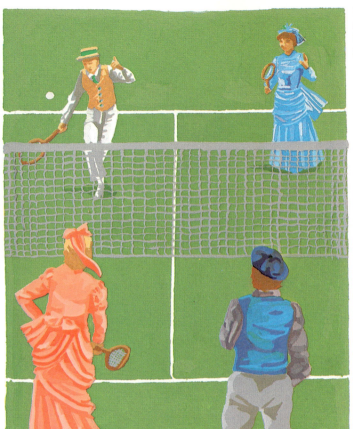

*The early days of Lawn Tennis: although it began as a social game for amusement, it quickly became a serious competitive sport.*

Lawn Tennis took its name from the lawns on which the first outdoor games of tennis were played in England in the 1870s. Real Tennis rackets were used in the first games of Lawn Tennis. The first rackets specially made for Lawn Tennis were introduced in 1874.

The first set of rules for Lawn Tennis was published in 1873 by Major Walter Wingfield. In 1875 tennis was played at the All England Croquet Club at Wimbledon and the rules for the modern game of tennis were established for the first Wimbledon tennis championships in 1877.

Today the rules of tennis are laid down by the International Tennis Federation, which is based in London. These rules are always devised in English in honour of the country where Lawn Tennis was born; but within a few years of its invention, tennis had become a popular sport all around the globe.

*Rackets through the ages: top, a Real Tennis racket; below, in descending order, Lawn Tennis rackets of the 1880s, 1930s and 1980s.*

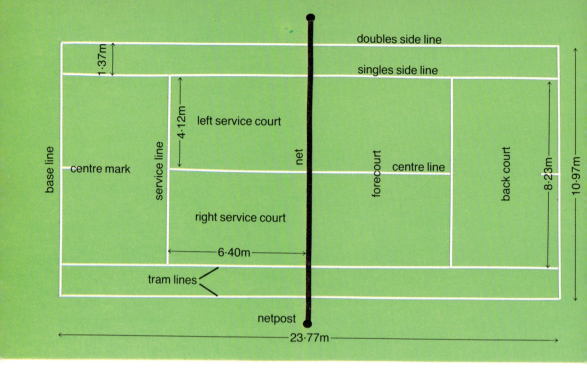

*The layout and dimensions of the court.*

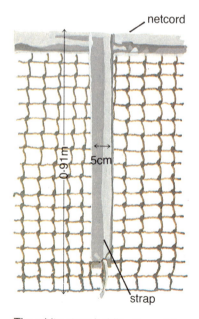

*The white strap holding the net firm at the centre of the court.*

# The court

Tennis courts are rectangular in shape. Lines are marked on the court with tape, paint or lime (chalk) to show where players have to stand and the areas of the court which are in play.

The court for a singles game is narrower than the court for a doubles game. The singles court is 23·77m x 8·23m. The doubles court measures 23·77m x 10·97m. (Note that all the original measurements for tennis were in feet and inches – for example, the doubles court was 78ft x 36ft. This is why the metric equivalents are not round numbers.)

The net extends across the centre of the court. It is almost a metre longer than the court at each side. It is 0·91m high and is held taut by a white strap which should not be more than 5cm wide.

The line at the back of the court is called the base line. There is a centre mark half way along it. The service line, half-way down the court, separates the back court from the forecourt. The forecourt is divided into right and left service courts.

The surface of a tennis court can be of grass, clay, cement, asphalt or tarmacadam. The various surfaces make the ball bounce in different ways and so demand different kinds of play.

A good grass court has a fast surface and so calls for quick reactions. Grass courts also need a lot of maintenance to keep them in good condition. Even then, weather conditions and general wear and tear can produce some awkward bounces. The tournaments at Wimbledon are played on grass courts.

*Grass was the original surface for Lawn Tennis. Because of the difficulties of maintaining grass courts and the unreliable bounce of the ball on them, more and more tennis clubs are turning to artificial surfaces.*

*'Rain stops play' – but not on an indoor court, where tennis can be played 365 days a year.*

Hard courts are more practical. Hard courts made of packed clay are used in the French Championships. Hard courts made of cement are used in the US Championships. Many hard courts, especially those in schools and public parks, are made of asphalt or tarmacadam.

Whereas most hard courts are smooth, hard courts made of clay have a topping of crushed brick, shale or stone. This topping reduces the speed of the bounce, which results in a slower game; players who do well on slow courts are good at tactical manoeuvring.

Other hard courts are usually medium to fast. Players can run more easily on these than on grass or clay, and the ball bounces more consistently.

Some courts have synthetic surfaces. These consist of a kind of thick carpet which is sometimes made to resemble grass very convincingly. The speed of such courts depends on the hardness of the surface on which the carpet has been laid.

Indoor courts have surfaces made of wood, or a layer of rubber placed on top of a harder surface.

# Preparing for play

Before beginning to play a game of tennis, the net must be adjusted to the right height. In games played amongst friends, or at local clubs, this is usually done by standing one racket vertically on the ground and placing the head of another racket sideways on top of it. The height of the net is adjusted by turning the netpost winder until the net is taut and then lowering it to the height of the rackets, or to 0·91m. Note that once the height of the net has been adjusted it must not be touched by a player or by his racket. If a player does touch the net during a game, he loses the point in play.

Players toss a coin for the right to choose which end of the court they would like to start playing from, or for the right to serve or receive the ball when the game begins. Traditionally the toss was done by twirling a racket: the coloured strings at the base of the head of a wooden racket feel 'rough' on one side and 'smooth' on the other, so could be used in the same way as the 'head' or 'tail' of a coin.

The player who wins the toss may choose to serve or receive first. His opponent then has the choice of ends from which to start playing. If the winner of the toss decides to choose ends, his opponent can choose to serve or receive first.

Players change ends after the first and third games, and following alternate games – when the total number of games played is an odd number.

Players usually have a warm-up session before play begins so that they can practise their strokes, including the service.

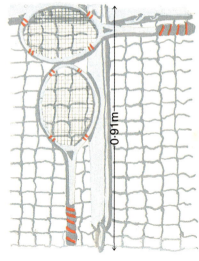

*The traditional way of measuring the net height: two rackets placed like this stand at approximately 0·91m.*

treblings
(smooth side up)

*Rough or smooth? All rackets used to have coloured strings, known as treblings, at the base of the head, which held the main strings in place.*

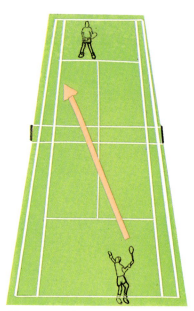

The service for the first point of a game.

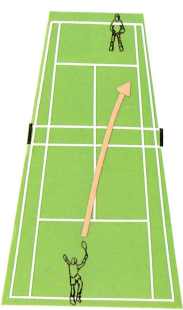

The service for the second point of a game.

# The service

Every point begins with a service. The server stands behind the base line. For the first point he stands to the right of the centre mark. He hits the ball over the net into the service court diagonally opposite. If the ball lands in the correct service court, bouncing here for the first time, it is 'good' (or 'in'). The server's opponent must return the ball after it has bounced once and before it bounces a second time.

To serve, the server can hit the ball underarm, or can throw it up into the air and hit it at full stretch. He can jump, but he must not run or walk to hit it, and he must not move his feet across the base line or the centre mark until he has hit the ball; if he does any of these a 'foot fault' will be called and the service is not allowed.

The service is not 'good' if the ball goes into the net, or goes over the net but lands outside the service court in play, if it touches the net and goes over it but lands outside the service court in play, or if the server does a foot fault. In any of these events a 'fault' is called and the server must try again.

The server is allowed two attempts to deliver a 'good' service for each point. If he makes a fault in both the first and the second service, this is called a 'double fault' and he loses the point.

After each point has been played, the server moves to the other side of the centre mark and his opponent moves to the other service court. The position of the server and receiver changes like this after each point. The receiver always receives the service in the service court diagonally opposite the server.

If when the ball is served it hits the net, goes over it and lands in the correct service court, a 'let' is called. The term 'let' comes from the use of the word let when it means 'to leave something alone'. If a let is called the server takes the service again. A let may also be called if the ball hits the net and then hits the receiver, or if the server begins to play before the receiver is ready.

Players take it in turns to serve: service alternates between the players at the end of each game until the end of the match. (In doubles the service rules are slightly different; see pages 16–17.)

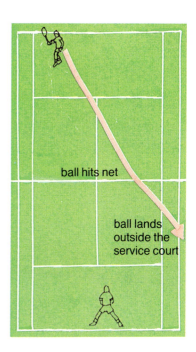

*Diagrams showing the service let rule. Above: the service is a fault. Below: the service is good.*

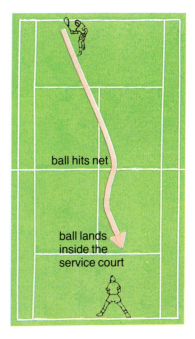

11

# The rally

Once the service is in, the ball is 'in play' and the receiver has to hit it back over the net into the server's court. Now the game begins in earnest. What follows is called a rally, with the players hitting the ball back and forth to each other until one makes a mistake or is unable to return the ball. A player will lose the point if:

- he fails to return a 'good' ball (one that lands inside his own court) before it bounces twice;
- he returns the ball so that it lands outside his opponent's court (in which case the ball is 'out').

There are other less obvious ways in which a point can be lost, such as if:

- a player touches the ball more than once with his racket before returning it to his opponent;
- a player hits the ball before it has crossed over to his side of the net;
- the ball in play touches any part of the player other than his racket.

A ball is 'good' if it bounces on the line of the court which is in play. It is sometimes difficult to judge whether a ball is in or out; this is one of the jobs of the umpire, or – in big tournaments – the separate line judges. In some tournaments electronic devices are used to check if the ball is in or out.

*In or out? Remember that if the ball bounces on the line it is counted as in.*

# Scoring

To win a tennis match a player must win a certain, specified number of *sets*; each set is made up of a number of *games*, and each game is made up of a number of *points*.

To win one of these games, a player must win four points. When a player has no points it is called 'love'. The first point is called 15, the second 30, the third 40.

The score of the server is always called first. If the server has one point and his opponent has two, the score is '15–30'. If both players have two points the score is '30 all'. If a player has a score of 40 and his opponent has a score of 15 or of 30, and he wins the next point, he wins that game and 'Game' is called.

If both players have 40, the score is called 'deuce'. At deuce one player must win two points in succession to win the game. If the server wins the next point it is called 'advantage server' (or 'advantage in'); if the receiver wins the next point it is called 'advantage receiver' (or 'advantage out'). If the other player then wins the next point the score returns to deuce. The game will not be won until one of the players wins the next point when the score is his advantage.

The words used for scoring in tennis are rather unusual. It is thought that the term deuce comes from the French *à deux*, meaning 'two points to go'; and that love, meaning no score, derives from *l'oeuf*, the French for egg, which is the shape of a zero. The other numbers used in scoring are thought to come from the quarters of the clock – 15, 30, 40 (a corruption of 45) – with 'Game' marking the hour.

egg – *l'oeuf* – love

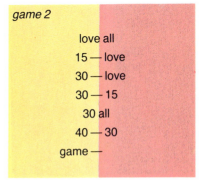

| server | receiver |
|---|---|
| *game 1* | |
| love all | |
| love — 15 | |
| love — 30 | |
| 15 — 30 | |
| 15 — 40 | |
| — game | |

| *game 2* | |
|---|---|
| love all | |
| 15 — love | |
| 30 — love | |
| 30 — 15 | |
| 30 all | |
| 40 — 30 | |
| game — | |

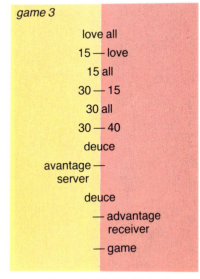

| *game 3* | |
|---|---|
| love all | |
| 15 — love | |
| 15 all | |
| 30 — 15 | |
| 30 all | |
| 30 — 40 | |
| deuce | |
| avantage — server | |
| deuce | |
| — advantage receiver | |
| — game | |

Above: examples of scoring in three games.
Left: the possible origins of the terms used in scoring.

The first player to win six games is the winner of the set, unless both players win five games each ('five games all'). In that case one of the players then has to win two games in a row to win the set (for example, 7–5, 8–6, 9–7, and so on). Alternatively, the tie-break system may be used, as explained on the next page.

A match usually consists of a maximum of three sets. This is called 'the best of three sets', meaning that the first player to reach two sets will win because, even if they play the third set, the opponent can still only win one set.

In some championships, such as Wimbledon, the winner of the men's matches is the one to win three sets out of five ('the best of five sets').

*The scoreboard showing the score during a tournament match. It is 15 all in the second set. Miss Dupont has won the first set by 7 games to 6 (following a tie-break), but Miss Baker has won the first game in the second set.*

*Concentration: the tie-break at the end of a long set can produce some nerve–racking tennis.*

| Player 1 | | Player 2 | |
|---|---|---|---|
| \multicolumn{4}{c}{six games all} | | | |
| serves | 1 | 0 | |
| | 1 | 1 | serves |
| | 1 | 2 | |
| serves | 2 | 2 | |
| | 3 | 2 | |
| | 4 | 2 | serves |
| | 5 | 2 | |
| serves | 6 | 2 | |
| | game | | |

| Player 1 | | Player 2 | |
|---|---|---|---|
| \multicolumn{4}{c}{six games all} | | | |
| serves | 1 | 0 | |
| | 1 | 1 | serves |
| | 1 | 2 | |
| serves | 2 | 2 | |
| | 3 | 2 | |
| | 3 | 3 | serves |
| | 3 | 4 | |
| serves | 4 | 4 | |
| | 5 | 4 | |
| | 5 | 5 | serves |
| | 5 | 6 | |
| serves | 6 | 6 | |
| | 7 | 6 | |
| | 7 | 7 | serves |
| | 7 | 8 | |
| serves | | game | |

To avoid extremely long sets, a 'tie-break' system is often introduced at six games all, provided that this has been agreed beforehand. A tie-break is a final, deciding game; the player who wins the tie-break wins the set.

The winner of a tie-break is the first player to win seven points, provided that he has two more points than his opponent. Numerical scoring – 1, 2, 3 etc. – is used in the tie-break. If the score reaches six points all, the tie-break will continue until one player scores two points in a row, putting him two clear points ahead of his opponent (8–6, 9–7, and so on).

The order of serving for the tie-break is as follows: the player whose turn it would normally be to serve in the next game serves for the first point; his opponent serves the second and third points. The players then alternate serves every two points until the end of the tie-break. They change ends after every six points.

The player who serves first in the tie-break game will receive first in the opening game of the next set.

*Examples of the score in two tie-break games. In the second game Player 2 only gets two points ahead at 9–7.*

15

# Doubles

The rules for doubles games of tennis are the same as for singles, except that there are four players and the area of the court in play is wider. This is because the outer areas on either side of the court (the 'tram lines') are used.

In preparing to play, the partners decide between themselves who will call the toss and who will serve first. Each player serves for one game with the service alternating between the pairs, so that each player serves once every fourth game (A, B, C, D in the diagram opposite). The partners must keep the same order of service for each set, but may change the order at the beginning of a new set.

The server stands behind the base line and between the centre mark and the tram lines to serve. He moves to the other side of the centre mark for the next point, and back again for the next, as in the singles game. The server's partner usually stands near to the net on the other side of the centre line for the service.

Positions for the service for the first point of a doubles game.

The server's opponents decide between them who will receive the serve first, and who second. The receiver who receives first does so for every game of that set. The order may be changed at the beginning of a new set. The player who is receiving the ball usually stands towards the back of the court, with his partner positioned towards the net, on the opposite side of the centre line.

If the service ball touches the server's partner, or his racket, before going over the net, the service is a fault. If it touches the receiver's partner, or his racket, before going back over the net, the receiver loses the point.

If a player serves when it should be his partner's turn to serve, the partner must serve for the rest of that game from the moment that the mistake is realised; the score stands unaltered. If a player receives in the wrong court, he stays in that court until the end of the game and then returns to the court that he should have been in.

Once the ball has been served and returned in a doubles game, either partner of a pair may return it when it is that pair's turn to do so, and points are won and lost in the same way as for the singles game.

*Although doubles matches receive less attention in professional tournaments, they can produce some of the most exhilarating tennis, with rapid shots flying back and forth between all four players.*

*From the umpire's chair the umpire has a good view of all the court.*

# Court officials

When players compete against friends, or in amateur tennis matches, they themselves usually keep the score and judge whether a ball is in or out and so forth.

In a tennis tournament an umpire is appointed to do this. The umpire sits in a raised seat at one end of the tennis net. From there he (or she) has a good view of the players and the court. He can see more clearly than any player and can make judgements about foot faults or lets. Players must accept the decision of an umpire without question.

In major international championships the umpire is helped by line judges (or linesmen), a netcord judge and a foot-fault judge. Line judges tell the umpire if a ball lands outside the court in play. The umpire will abide by the call of the line judges unless he feels that the call is wrong, in which case he can overrule the decision of a line judge.

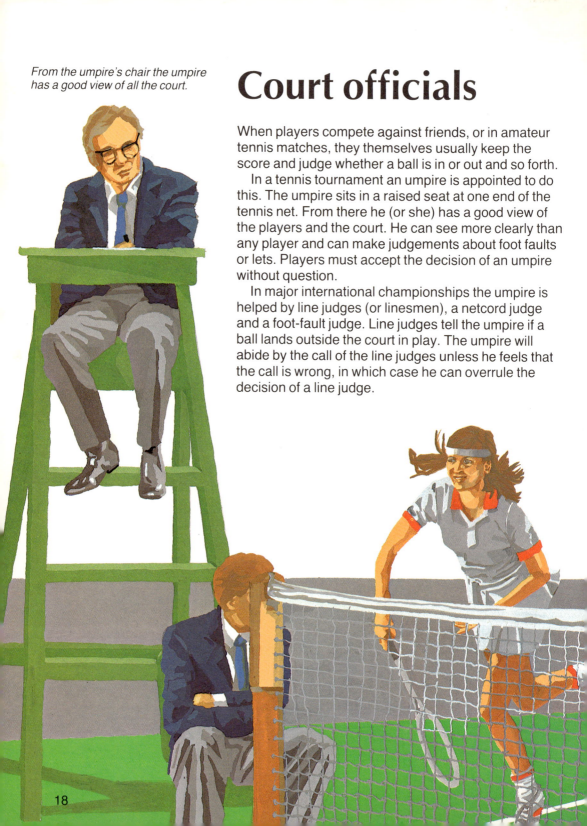

*The netcord judge sits with his finger on the netcord during the service. If the ball touches the net he can feel the vibrations in the netcord. Here he is assisted by a sensitive electronic device.*

The netcord judge sits close to one end of the net, with a finger on the net, so that he can hear and feel if the ball hits the net during the service. This is important, for if the ball hits the net during a service and goes into the service court a 'let' must be called.

The foot-fault judge has to watch the server's feet and make a call if they cross the base line or the centre mark before the server hits the ball.

Sometimes a referee is appointed to a major tennis competition. He controls the tournament and arranges the order of play (who will play against whom). In the event of a dispute he can be consulted on points of tennis law by the umpires. If any player behaves badly, the referee can report him to his national tennis association.

In most major tennis championships six ball boys or ball girls are present on court. They stand or kneel – ready to run for the balls – beside the court, behind the base line and at the net. They collect the balls from the court and make sure the server has two balls to serve with. Ball boys and ball girls must be able to carry out their task without distracting the players. They have to be very quiet and nimble on their feet.

*Ball boys and ball girls have an essential task in big tournaments. It is one of those jobs which is only really noticed if it is not done well.*

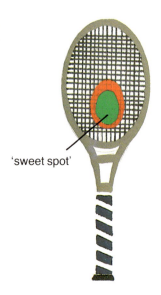

'sweet spot'

*A diagram showing the area on a racket known as the 'sweet spot', with which the ball can be hit to most effect.*

# Equipment

## Rackets

The most important piece of equipment in the game of tennis is the tennis racket. A tennis racket can be of any shape or weight, but must not be longer than 81.28cm (32 inches) or wider than 31.75cm (12½ inches). The weight and shape of the racket that a player chooses will depend on his age and size. Younger players will find it easier to play with a racket which is light and has a short handle.

Most senior players use rackets which weigh between 335g and 350g. Some players today choose rackets which have large heads to increase the size of the area on the strings which is known as the 'sweet spot'. The sweet spot is the best place on the racket with which to return the ball.

*Rackets can be any shape or size provided that they are not larger than the maximum size as stated in the rules. Young players usually start with smaller rackets.*

The size of the circumference of the grip is important. The usual grip sizes are 11·7cm to 12·7cm for men, and 11·4cm to 12·1cm for women.

Racket frames are traditionally made of wood. Today, however, most frames are made of graphite or other materials, such as aluminium, steel, plastic and glass fibre. These are usually longer lasting than frames made of wood, which may warp if they are not kept in cool, dry conditions.

Racket strings can be made of natural 'gut' (now usually twisted cattle hide) or of nylon, or of a mixture of the two. Strings made of natural gut break less easily than synthetic strings, but gut is more expensive and can be affected by wet and damp weather.

The tension of the strings of a racket can vary. Players who hit the ball very hard prefer tightly strung rackets. Players who specialise in ball control prefer looser strings so that the ball stays momentarily longer on the racket. This gives them a chance to twist or turn the racket as they hit the ball in order to put a spin on it.

*The parts of a tennis racket.*

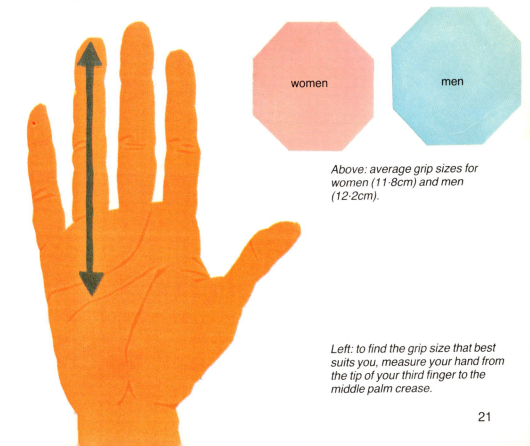

*Above: average grip sizes for women (11·8cm) and men (12·2cm).*

*Left: to find the grip size that best suits you, measure your hand from the tip of your third finger to the middle palm crease.*

# Tennis balls

Tennis balls measure between 6·35cm and 6·67cm across the middle. They weigh between 56·7g and 58·5g. Most tennis balls have a pressurised rubber core; they are covered with a furry cloth, or 'knap', made from a mixture of wool and nylon and coloured yellow or white. The air pressure inside the balls is varied for different conditions. Hard, fast balls are more suitable for slower courts. Softer, slower balls are more suitable for faster courts.

Manufacturers of tennis balls test their bounce very carefully. The balls must bounce more than 135cm and less than 147cm when dropped from a height of 254cm onto a concrete base. In championship games, balls are changed frequently to ensure that the correct bounce is maintained.

*Tennis balls may be either yellow or white. The interior of a tennis ball consists of two hemispheres of black rubber.*

*Many people bounce the ball before serving. This is not just to help their concentration, but also to check the ball's bounce.*

*Protect your rackets with a racket cover. Some covers protect the head only, others the whole racket, or even two or three rackets. Soft travelling bags are excellent for carrying your equipment around in.*

## Care of equipment

It is important to look after your tennis equipment. Tennis rackets should be kept in cool, dry conditions. You should protect your racket from rain or damage when not in use with a racket cover – but it is not advisable to keep the racket cover on when the racket is being stored for some time as this might cause condensation. For older wooden rackets, which are prone to warping, a racket press is essential.

It is a good idea to keep tennis balls in a refrigerator: this ensures that they have a consistent bounce when played.

Players should also look after the tennis court itself, taking trouble not to damage the surface in any way. After a match, the net should be lowered to take the tension off the netcord, the white strap should be unclipped from its anchor in the ground, and the lower part of the net should be placed over the net to keep it off the ground. If this is not done, wet weather will soon damage the net, and the foot of the net will fray in the wind.

*Remember always to lower the net and hang it over the netcord at the end of the day.*

*Tennis wear from the beginning of the century.*

# Tennis clothes

Clothing for playing tennis must be cool and comfortable and able to absorb sweat. It should be loose enough to allow free movement, but not so loose as to get in the way of play.

Fashions for tennis clothes change from year to year. Early tennis players wore clothes specially made for the game, but they were considerably fuller and heavier than the clothes worn for tennis today. Today's tennis clothes are more practical.

*Tennis clothes have to be light and loose enough to remain comfortable throughout a long match. These players are shaking hands at the end of a match – the traditional way to thank your opponent for the game.*

Men and boys usually wear shorts and short-sleeved shirts; women and girls usually wear skirts and shirts, or tennis dresses. Tennis clothing is generally white, although coloured symbols and decorations are increasingly common.

It is important to wear comfortable shoes and socks. Special tennis socks cushion and protect the feet from rubbing against the shoes. Tennis shoes should provide firm support under the foot and should have soles which grip the surface of the court well.

Some tennis players wear head and wrist bands made of towelling to keep the sweat out of their eyes and off their hands.

*Tennis shoes should fit snugly. When buying a pair pay special attention to the grip marks on the soles.*

*At full stretch: your tennis will be impaired if your clothes obstruct your movements in any way.*

25

# The strokes

The greater the variety of strokes a player can use in a rally, the greater are his chances of winning. The two main ways of hitting the ball are the forehand and backhand strokes.

The forehand is used to return balls approaching right-handed players on the right-hand side, and left-handed players on the left-hand side. The backhand is used for returning balls approaching right-handed players on the left-hand side, and left-handed players on the right-hand side.

Although there are some very famous left-handed tennis players, most players are right-handed. The instructions about strokes in this book, therefore, will be given as if you, the reader, are right-handed. If you are left-handed, you will have to reverse right and left in these instructions to apply them to you.

*The forehand drive (left) and backhand drive (right).*

# The grips

For all strokes the way that you grip the racket is important. The most widely used grip for the forehand is the Eastern forehand grip. Place the palm of the right hand against the racket strings. Hold the racket out in front of you with the left hand at the 'neck' of the racket (where the handle meets the racket head) to do this. Keep the strings vertical to the ground and the handle pointing to the stomach. Draw the right hand down to the handle of the racket. Wrap the fingers and thumb around the handle as if you were shaking someone's hand. The V between the fingers and the thumb should be on top of the racket handle.

To find the backhand grip, hold the racket in the right hand with the forehand grip, and with the left hand at the neck. Twist the right hand round to the left. Place the thumb straight up the back of the racket handle, or diagonally across it. The V between the finger and thumb should be on the top left side of the handle.

*The grips: top two, the forehand; lower two, the backhand.*

*The forehand drive.*

1

## Ground strokes

The basic strokes for returning a ball are the ground strokes, so-called because they are played after the ball has hit the ground. Forehand ground strokes are called forehand drives; backhand ground strokes are called backhand drives.

### The forehand drive

To return a ball with a forehand drive, use a forehand grip and begin to swing the racket back as the ball approaches. Turn sideways to the right and begin to step forwards onto your left foot. Swing your racket round to the front as the ball bounces and step onto your left foot just before you hit the ball.

Remember to keep the face of the racket vertical during the swing, so that you do not lose control of the direction of the shot. Aim to hit the ball when it is between knee and waist height. Once the ball has left your racket, continue to swing the racket in the direction of the ball (this is called 'following through'). If the ball bounces low, bend your knees to hit it. Keep your eyes on the ball all the time you are playing your shot.

1  2  3

## The backhand drive
To return the ball with a backhand drive, hold the neck of the racket with the left hand and change to the backhand grip. Turn from facing the net to the left, until you are standing sideways to the net. Hold the racket head slightly above wrist level. Continue to hold the racket with both hands as you start to move it towards the ball. Step from the back (left) foot on to the front (right) foot, and let go of the racket with the left hand. Stretch your arm and hit the ball. Bend your knees and keep your wrist stiff as you hit the ball. Follow the ball through with your racket as you did in the forehand drive.

Some players these days use a two-handed backhand stroke, holding the racket with both hands until the ball has been hit. This makes a more powerful stroke, but it also means that you cannot stretch so far to reach the ball.

Length and direction are important in forehand and backhand drives. It is more difficult for your opponent to score a winning shot if your returns are aimed to bounce near his base line; and good, hard shots placed out of your opponent's reach will be winners. It is the strength of your swing that gives the ball its speed, and your follow-through will help to give it direction.

*Above: the backhand drive.
Below: the double-handed backhand drive.*

29

## The service

The service (or serve) is the most important stroke of the game. A player with a strong service can sometimes win many points by serving balls which his opponent is quite unable to return. Such serves are called 'aces'.

Some players use an underarm service when they first begin to play. To serve in this way the player stands behind the base line and to the correct side of the centre mark and then hits the ball with a forehand drive.

Beginners should, however, move on to the simple overhead service as soon as possible. The grip for this kind of service is the same as for the forehand drive. Stand behind the base line and sideways to it. With the ball held against the strings, point your racket at the service court. Move your arms upwards, placing the ball up in the air with your left hand. Hit the ball square on, towards the service court.

*The simple service.*

1    2

*The advanced service.*

When you have mastered the simple service you can go on to use the advanced service. This is the same as the simple service except that you swing your arm and racket back and upwards, and hit the ball with a throwing action. For this you should use the backhand grip. The wrist remains loose as you hit the ball, and is used to give an extra flick to the racket.

The advanced service gives much more power to the serve and allows you to put spin on the ball so that it curves away from your opponent as it flies through the air. The most important thing about serving, however, is to get the ball in. There is little point in developing a powerful service if it only results in a string of double faults!

Be careful also not to lose your service point by making foot faults. Keep your feet behind the base line and to the side of the centre mark until you have hit the ball.

## The volley

The volley is an attacking stroke. It is different from a ground stroke because the ball does not bounce before it is hit. It is usually played from close to the net.

The volley requires almost no backswing: it uses the speed of the oncoming ball to make a return with a short, punching gesture.

### The forehand volley

As the ball comes towards you, turn sideways and step forwards with your left foot. Lean towards the net. Keep your eye on the ball. Use the racket as if you were catching the ball. Do not swing it behind you. When the ball touches the racket strings, push it away with a firm punch of the racket. Keep your wrist locked. Your weight should be on your left foot as you hit the ball. Use your left arm to help you keep your balance.

*The forehand volley.*

## The backhand volley
Use the backhand drive grip. Hold the neck of the racket with your left hand and keep the racket head high. Step forward with your right foot. Keep the racket out in front of you. If the ball is a low one, bend your knees. Keep your back straight. Do not swing your racket back. If the ball is quite high, swing your racket slightly. Use the same punching movement to hit the ball as you did for the forehand volley, releasing the racket with the left hand to do so.

## The half-volley
You can use the half-volley just after the ball has bounced. Keep your eye on the ball and aim to play it low over the net. Try to place it away from your opponent – in singles, down the side line; in doubles, between your opponents. The half-volley can produce some of the fastest and most effective shots in tennis.

*Above: leaping for a high backhand volley.*
*Left: a backhand volley at shoulder height.*

33

*The overhead smash.*

## The lob

The lob is a good shot to use when your opponent is standing close to the net. It goes high and a long way out of the reach of your opponent's racket. You should aim a lob at your opponent's base line.

You can make a lob with a forehand or a backhand stroke. Use the same grip and footwork as for the forehand and backhand drives. Try to position the lob so that, if your opponent does manage to run back to it, he has to play it with a backhand.

## The drop shot

Use a forehand or backhand stroke to drop the ball softly just over the net. This stroke is best used when your opponent is standing at the back of the court and you are standing close to the net.

## The overhead smash

This stroke is useful if you want to return a lob. It is a similar stroke to the advanced service. Aim to hit the ball when it is high. Lift your racket and drop the head over your shoulder. Try to keep your feet on the ground, but if you have to jump, jump off your back (right) foot and land on your front (left) foot.

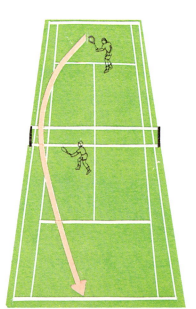
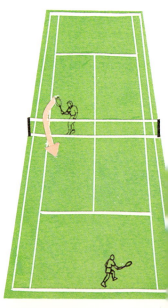

*The lob (left) and the drop shot (right).*

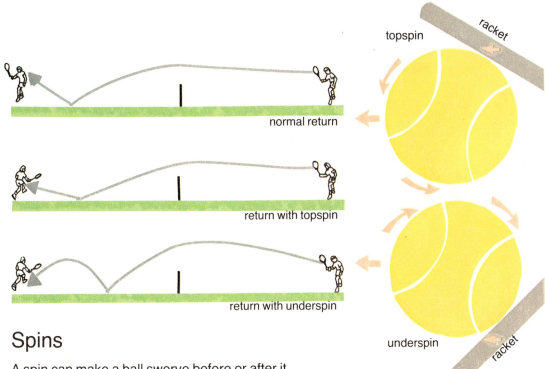

## Spins

A spin can make a ball swerve before or after it bounces, or skid, or slow down on hitting the ground. Spins need a delicate touch, and you can only learn these techniques with practice, but they are very effective ways of making the ball more difficult for your opponent to return.

### Topspin
Topspin makes the ball rise higher than it does with a normal flat forehand or backhand stroke, but on landing it bounces lower. To give a ball topspin, roll the racket over the top of the ball as you hit it.

### Underspin
Underspin (also called backspin) makes the ball float through the air more than it would do with the normal forehand or backhand strokes, but when it lands it has a much shorter bounce. To give a ball underspin, hit it below its centre line, with the racket at a slight slant.

### Slice
Slice is produced by hitting across the direction of the ball, making it swerve as it flies through the air. It can be used very effectively to direct the ball away from your opponent's reach, especially in the service.

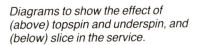

*Diagrams to show the effect of (above) topspin and underspin, and (below) slice in the service.*

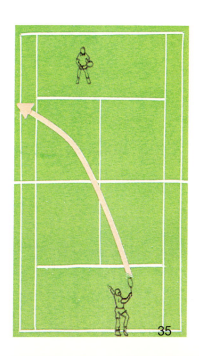

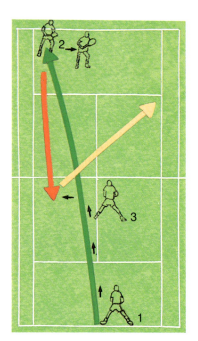

*A diagram of the winning tactics of a serve-and-volley specialist.*

# Tactics

You can improve your tennis by thinking about your tactics. By planning the way that you play your shots you can create space on the court into which you can aim a winning shot, or pressurise your opponent into making a mistake, or to change the speed of the game in order to take your opponent by surprise.

Good tennis players fall into two main categories: serve-and-volley specialists and base-line players. Serve-and-volley specialists concentrate on making their service powerful, and move to the net after they have served so that they can smash any returns into their opponent's court. These tactics are best for fast courts.

Base-line players stay at the back of the court and play long, accurate shots, waiting to make a winning shot or to force an error from their opponent. Slower courts are more suitable for base-line players.

It is best for beginners to practise both these approaches.

*The serve-and-volley specialist follows up an attacking service by running to the net, ready to volley any returns.*

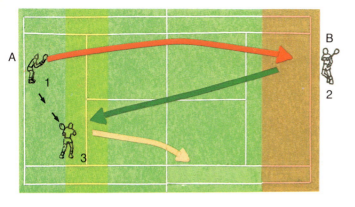

By playing a good-length ball (into the brown zone), Player A keeps his opponent at the back of the court. Player B opens himself up for attack by playing a poor-length ball (into the yellow zone), which Player A steers away to a winner with a drop shot.

## Creating spaces

The skill of creating the space to play a winning shot usually depends on being able to vary the length and direction of your shots. In general the nearer your ball lands to the net, the easier it is for your opponent to return a winning shot. Try to make a ball land near the base line, even if it means hitting the ball high over the net. Make up your mind as quickly as possible where you want the ball to land and aim your racket in that direction. Keep your head down and follow the ball through.

## Pressurising your opponent

Pressurise your opponent into making an error either by placing each shot in a different part of the court each time you hit it, or by playing a long rally, placing the ball in the same spot time and again until you suddenly change direction.

## Changing speed

The speed of your shot depends not only on how hard you hit it and how fast the ball is coming at you, but also on how much you lean into the ball and how much of your weight moves forward as you hit it.

Clearly a hard, fast shot can beat your opponent by sheer speed, but soft shots, such as drop shots and lobs, can be every bit as effective. Vary your play and learn as many strokes as possible – and keep your opponent guessing.

*Taking her time and using plenty of backswing, this player can keep her opponent guessing until the moment she plays the shot.*

37

*Above: getting a partner to throw balls to you provides excellent, controlled practice.*
*Below: practising throwing the ball for the service – without hitting it.*

# Practice

## Racket action

### Forehand and backhand action
Practise forehand and backhand drives by hitting a ball against a wall, or by returning a ball thrown to you by a partner. Concentrate particularly on developing a smooth, flowing style with plenty of backswing and follow-through. Practise aiming the ball accurately.

### Service action
To practise the racket action for the serve, try throwing some balls, overarm, to reach the far end of the court without bouncing. Keep your feet fixed on the ground as you do this. Now practise the same action with your racket in your hand.

 A very important part of the service action is the way that you place the ball in the air to hit it. To practise this, stand sideways to the net, lift the ball with your arm straight, thrusting it gently upwards, then let it fall to the ground – without hitting it. It should land just in front of your left toe. Repeat this exercise until you can get it right ten times in succession.

# Racket control

### Control in ground strokes
You can practise the forehand and backhand strokes when you are practising your racket actions against a wall or with a partner. Remember to use the correct grips.

When practising with a partner on court, choose an area of the court where you are going to aim your shots. Practise returning balls to each other at the spots you have chosen. One of you can practise the forehand, always placing the ball to the other's backhand; then you can reverse the roles.

### Service control
Using the service grip, use the racket to bounce the ball one hundred times on the ground. When you can do this with ease, place four markers on the ground, about one metre apart from each other. Bounce the ball in the same way, moving in and out of the markers.

Practise serving at targets in the service courts. The most effective spots at which to aim your serve are the two rear corners of the service court, those that are nearest to your opponent.

### Control in the volley
With a partner, take turns for one to use a ground stroke and the other to return it with a volley from the net. See how long you can keep up a rally with both of you volleying.

### Control of the lob and the smash
The lob and the smash can be practised together, with one player sending a lob to be returned with a smash by the other.

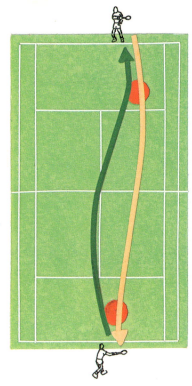

*Practising forehand and backhand strokes with a partner, each always aiming for the same spot on the court.*

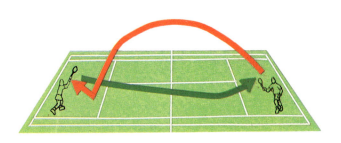

*Two players practising the lob and the smash at the same time.*

*Running, picking up balls, turning, running back: this 'potato race' exercise strengthens your leg muscles and improves your acceleration.*

# Training

There are a number of training exercises that you can use to help you to improve your tennis. To play good tennis you need to be able to run fast, stop or change directions suddenly, accelerate quickly, and bend, twist and stretch with your body.

Strong leg muscles will help you to do this. Practise squats, as follows. Stand with your feet a little apart and your back straight, arms raised horizontally in front of you. Bend your knees until your thighs are nearly parallel with the ground, no lower, breathing in as you do this. Push yourself up quickly, keeping your head up and breathing out.

Improve your acceleration and control on court by practising changing speeds as you run. Start at jogging speed. After ten paces, change to a sprint, running as fast as you can on your toes for a further ten paces. Alternate the two as you make your way around the court.

Put a line of tennis balls on the court at different distances from the base line. Run to pick up the nearest ball and return it to the base line. Turn quickly and collect the second ball and return that to the base line. Continue doing this until you have returned all the balls. Time yourself, and see if you can improve your performance each time you do this exercise.

*Push-ups using the thigh and calf muscles.*

The power in running lies in the push-off with the back foot in each stride. To improve your mobility and your turn of speed, practise running using shorter and shorter strides. Then practise running using longer strides. Run around the court counting the number of strides that you use, and then run around the court several times more, each time using fewer strides.

Practise fast skipping on the spot.

Improving your balance will help you to reach further to hit a ball. Practise running fast about the court with your racket, making strokes to hit imaginary balls as you do so. Remember the correct footwork and grips for the strokes, and to use plenty of swing. (You may think that this looks silly, but it is a good training tactic, used by professionals.)

Practising hip turns is also good for your balance. Stand with your feet apart and your right hand on your right hip. Put the other arm behind your neck, holding the right shoulder with your hand, with the thumb to the front. Keep this position and turn from right to left twenty times without losing balance. Now reverse this position and repeat the exercise.

By practising these training exercises you will become faster and more sure-footed. When doing the exercises always bear in mind the aspects of your game that can be improved through them.

## Five tips for better play

- Keep your back straight and your weight over both your feet while you are waiting for the ball. Stay on your toes, especially when waiting for your opponent to return the ball.
- Watch your opponent carefully. Anticipate his return and be prepared to run to receive it.
- Try to disguise your shots.
- Be patient: wait for good opportunities to score points.
- Make sure you have a good mental attitude: concentrate on the game and think positively about your play.

*Skipping.*

*Hip-turning.*

# Professional tennis

## Organisations

Tennis is becoming more and more popular with every passing year. The big international tournaments attract not only huge crowds but also millions of television viewers throughout the world. Professional tennis has become big business making the successful few into stars – and extremely rich.

The international championships represent the tip of a vast pyramid of competitions that take place throughout the world, from the local club tournaments to regional and national championships upwards. All these have to be carefully planned and organised at all levels.

There are several organisations which look after the affairs of tennis at the international level. The supreme governing body for the game is the International Tennis Federation (ITF). One hundred and eight countries belong to the ITF. The Federation is responsible for the rules of tennis. It runs the top team competitions, such as the Davis Cup and the Federation Cup, and it lends its approval to the official championships, such as the Wimbledon Tournament. It also promotes the game at international level and arranges training courses for players in different countries.

*The Wimbledon men's singles trophy.*

*An aerial view of the All England Club where the Wimbledon Championships are played.*

# The international championships

There are four main international championships held every year. The Australian Championships are played at the National Tennis Centre, Flinders Park, Melbourne, in January. The French Championships are played at the Roland Garros stadium, Paris, in May–June. The All England Championships are held at Wimbledon during June–July. The US Championships are held at Flushing Meadow, New York, in August–September.

These are all Open Championships, which means that both amateur and professional players from all countries can enter them.

Being the champion of all four of these tournaments at the same time is known as the Grand Slam. For most international tennis stars, winning the Grand Slam is the greatest achievement they can aspire to. Only six singles players have done this: Donald Budge in 1938, Maureen Connolly in 1953, Rod Laver in 1962 and 1969, Margaret Court in 1970, Martina Navratilova in 1983–84, and Steffi Graf in 1988.

# Seeding

Seeding is the system used in tennis championships whereby leading tennis players are placed in the draw so that they do not play against each other until the later stages of the tournament. The best players are known as 'top seeds'. It is unusual, though not impossible, for them to be knocked out in the early rounds by unseeded players.

*Above:* Martina Navratilova holding up the Wimbledon women's singles trophy.
*Below:* a chart showing a simple order of play for a tournament.

*The Davis Cup.*

## Team events

Tennis is not all about individuals: there are also international team events which attract top-class players who are honoured to be asked to represent their country in the national team.

The Davis Cup was established in 1900 in the USA when Dwight Davis, who was US doubles champion, gave a cup for the competition. It is played annually by men's teams from various countries of the world. Each team consists of two doubles players and two singles players who take part in a total of five matches, four singles and one doubles.

The women's equivalent of the Davis Cup is the Federation Cup, established in 1963 by the International Lawn Tennis Federation. Each team plays two singles matches and a doubles match.

Another important women's team event is the Wightman Cup. It was first played in 1923 and is between the USA and Great Britain. It consists of seven matches, five singles and two doubles.

The King's Cup is a competition for European teams. It is called the King's Cup because the trophy was donated in 1936 by King Gustav V of Sweden, himself a keen tennis player.

*The big tournaments and major team events draw huge crowds.*

# Junior championships

The great champions were all juniors once: every year there are new young players coming up through the ranks and reaching an outstanding professional level at an early age. These players begin like everyone else, playing and winning at local and school tournaments, gradually working their way up to more important regional and national tournaments.

There are several international championships for junior players, entry to which is restricted by age: under 14, under 16, under 18 and so forth. The Junior Hardcourt Championships of Great Britain, also known as Junior Wimbledon, are played in June–July of each year, and many of the past winners have gone on to be great professional players.

But it is not an easy life. Junior champions have to work tirelessly and with great dedication to achieve their goals. Many of them start when they are very young; these days they may begin learning their skills with indoor Short Tennis before moving on to the real thing.

If you are not a dedicated champion, do not worry! Tennis is meant to be fun – but it will be more fun if you take the trouble to practise and to learn more skills, and always aim to play a better game.

*Starting young: Short Tennis is played indoors on a small court, with plastic rackets and a foam ball. It is proving to be an increasingly popular way to introduce children to tennis.*

*Stefan Edberg holding the Junior Wimbledon trophy, which he won in 1983. He went on to win the Wimbledon men's singles trophy in 1988.*

# Facts and figures

- Tennis might have been called 'Sphairistiké': this was the name that Major Wingfield wanted to give it when he wrote the rules of the game in 1873.

- The youngest champion ever was Charlotte 'Lottie' Dod of Great Britain, who was 15 years and 285 days when she won Wimbledon for the first time in 1887.

- Boris Becker became the youngest men's champion ever when he won Wimbledon for the first time in 1986 aged 17 years and 227 days.

- The youngest player to compete at Wimbledon in modern times was Tracey Austin, who was 14 years and 6 months when she played there in 1977. She became the youngest women's champion of this century when she won the US singles title in 1979 aged 16 years and 271 days.

- At each Wimbledon Tournament approximately 590 matches are played, 14,400 balls are used, and there are 270 umpires.

- After a gap of sixty-four years tennis became an official Olympic sport again at the 1988 Olympic Games held in Seoul, South Korea.

- The first great left-handed player was Dwight Davis, the American doubles player who donated the Davis Cup. Other famous left-handed players include Martina Navratilova (USA), John McEnroe (USA) and Jimmy Connors (USA).

- Many of the great tennis champions have used the two-handed back-hand. They include: Bjorn Borg, Jimmy Connors, Tracey Austin and Chrissie Evert.

- The fastest service ever officially measured was delivered by 'Big Bill' Tilden in 1931. It was timed at 263 kilometres per hour. In 1981 a coach called Horst Goepper claimed to have served a ball at 337 kilometres per hour during a test at Weinheim, West Germany.

- The longest set on record was played between Margaret Court and Billie Jean King in 1970 at Wimbledon: it lasted 2 hours and 26 minutes and was finally won by Margaret Court with the score at 14 games to 12.

- The longest game on record took place in a championship in Surrey in 1975. There were 37 deuces and 80 points and the game lasted 31 minutes.

- Fashions have changed. When the seventeen-year-old player May Sutton rolled up her sleeves and exposed her wrists at the 1905 Wimbledon Championships, the audience was shocked by her 'unladylike' behaviour. She went on to win the tournament.

- There are numerous dramatic tales surrounding the Davis Cup. In 1938 Czechoslovakia was declared the loser against Yugoslavia when one of their players, Franz Cejnar, was locked into his dressing room during a break for bad light by someone who went off with the key, preventing him from being able to return to the court.

- Tennis champions are now the world's highest-paid sportsmen and women. Top champions earn millions of dollars in prize money, but will also earn up to ten times as much again from sponsorship by the many companies which they help to advertise.

# Glossary

**ace:** a service which the receiver is unable to return.
**amateur:** a player who receives no money for playing tennis.
**back court:** the area between the service line and the base line.
**base line:** the line which marks the rear edge of the court and behind which the server must stand.
**break point:** a point in which the receiver is within one point of winning the game. This is an important moment in good tennis, because the server is usually expected to win the game.
**dink:** a very gently hit shot, usually played across the court.
**double fault:** the failure of two consecutive services to land in the correct service court, which results in the server losing that point.
**drop shot:** a gentle shot which lands just over the net, usually hit with underspin so that it has a reduced bounce.
**forecourt:** the area between the service line and the net.
**Grand Slam:** being the holder of the four major championships at the same time: the Wimbledon, the United States, the French and the Australian Championships.
**ground stroke:** a stroke that is played after the ball has bounced.
**in play:** a ball is in play from the moment the server hits it until an error is made and the point is scored.
**let:** 'let' is called when a ball hits the net in a service and goes into the correct service court, or when there is a disturbance which affects the players. The point is replayed, including two services unless the let is called because the ball hit the net in the second service, in which case only one service is replayed.
**lob:** a soaring shot which travels high over the head of an opponent and lands near the base line.

**match point:** a point in which one player is within one point of winning the match.
**percentage tennis:** taking no risks with the shots played, but playing only shots in which there is a high chance of success.
**poach:** in doubles, when a player hits a ball when it would normally be expected to be played by his partner.
**professional:** a player who earns money from playing tennis.
**rally:** all the shots between the service and and the shot which wins the point.
**receiver:** the player who is to receive the service.
**scrambling:** running to return a ball which looks as though it is unreachable.
**seed:** one of a number of players who are judged to be the strongest contenders in a tournament and who are given selected positions in the the order of play so that they do not play against each other in the early rounds.
**service winner:** a service which is good enough to prevent a return although the opponent does manage to hit it.
**set point:** a point in which one player is within one point of winning the set.
**side line:** the lines that mark the outer edge of the court in play, running the length of the court. For singles the side lines are the inner tram lines on either side; for doubles, the outer tram lines.
**smash:** the attacking shot which uses a stroke similar to the advanced serve to return a lob.
**spin:** the effect on the ball when the racket is used to cause the ball to swerve, skid, slow down on bouncing, or to bounce high or low.
**stroke:** the action of hitting the ball.
**tram lines:** the lines running along both sides of the court which mark the areas used in doubles games, but not in singles.
**volley:** a stroke played in returning the ball before it has hit the ground.

# Index

ace, 30, 47
back court, 6, 47
backhand, 26, 27, 28, 29, 33, 34, 35, 38, 39, 46
backspin, 35
backswing, 32, 37, 38
ball (size, manufacture), 22–3
ball boy/ball girl, 19
base line, 6, 11, 16, 19, 30, 31, 36, 37, 47
break point, 47
centre line, 6, 16, 17
centre mark, 6, 11, 16, 19, 30, 31
clothes, 24–5
court, (size) 6; (surface) 7–8; (care of) 23
double fault, 11, 31, 47
doubles, 3, 6, 16–17, 44, 47
drop shot, 34, 37, 47
fault, 11
following through, 28, 29, 38
foot fault, 11, 18, 31
foot-fault judge, 18, 19
forecourt, 6, 47
forehand, 26, 27, 28, 29, 30, 32, 34, 35, 38, 39
game (in scoring), 13–15, 46
Grand Slam, 43, 47
grass court, 7
grip (holding the racket), 27, 30, 31, 34, 39, 41
grip (part of racket), 21

ground stroke, 28–9, 32, 39, 47
half-volley, 33
hard court, 8
indoor court, 2, 4, 8
International Tennis Federation, 5, 42
*Jeu de Paume*, 4
knap, 22
let, 11, 18, 19, 47
line judge, 12, 18
lob, 34, 37, 39, 47
match point, 47
net, (size) 6; (height) 9; (care of) 23
netcord, 6, 19, 23
netcord judge, 18–19
netpost, 6
netpost winder, 9
Olympic Games, 46
order of play, 19, 43
percentage tennis, 47
point (in scoring), 13–15
practice, 38–9
professional tennis, 2, 42–3, 47
racket, (history) 4–5; (size) 20–1; (strings) 20–1; (care of) 23
racket cover, 23
racket press, 23
rally, 12, 26, 37, 39, 47
Real Tennis, 4–5

referee, 19
scoring, 13–15
scrambling, 47
seed, 43, 47
serve-and-volley, 36
service, 9, 10, 11, 12, 16, 17, 19, 30–1, 35, 36, 38, 39, 46, 47
service court, 6, 11, 19, 30, 39, 47
service line, 6, 47
set, 13–15, 16, 17, 46
set point, 47
shoes, 25
Short Tennis, 45
side line, 6, 33, 47
singles, 3, 6, 16, 17, 44, 47
slice, 35
smash, 34, 39, 47
spin, 21, 31, 35, 47
strings (stringing; types of), 20–1
sweet spot, 20
swing, 28, 29, 41
tie break, 14, 15
topspin, 35
toss, 9, 16
tram lines, 6, 16, 47
treblings, 9
umpire, 12, 18, 19, 46
underspin, 35, 47
volley, 32–3, 36, 39, 47
warm-up, 9

---

British Library Cataloguing in Publication Data
Dawson, Linda
   Tennis
   I. Lawn tennis
   I. Title II. Baranov, Liz III. Series
   796.342
   ISBN 0-7451-5084-5

Printed in Great Britain

A Cherrytree Book

First published 1990
by Cherrytree Press Ltd
a subsidiary of
The Chivers Company Ltd
Windsor Bridge Road
Bath, Avon, BA2 3AX

Copyright © Librairie du Liban 1990
All rights reserved